THE
HOPE
PRAYER

THE
HOPE
PRAYER

WORDS TO NOURISH THE SOUL

LIAM
LAWTON

HACHETTE
BOOKS
IRELAND

Copyright © Liam Lawton 2009

First published in 2009 by Hachette Books Ireland

The right of Liam Lawton to be identified as the Author
of the Work has been asserted by him in accordance with
the Copyright, Designs and Patents Act, 1988.

1

A CIP catalogue record for this title is available from the
British Library.

ISBN 978 0 340 96396 8

Typeset in Sabon 13pt by Sin É Design
Cover and interior design by Sin É Design
Printed and bound by Clays Ltd, St Ives plc.

Hachette Books Ireland policy is to use papers that are
natural, renewable and recyclable products and made
from wood grown in sustainable forests. The logging and
manufacturing processes are expected to conform to the
environmental regulations of the country of origin.

Hachette Books Ireland
8 Castlecourt Centre
Castleknock
Dublin 15, Ireland

A division of Hachette UK Ltd
338 Euston Road, London NW1 3BH, England

www.hbgi.ie

CONTENTS

For Niamh,
whose courage calls hope
into life

FOREWORD

Many people will wake up today realising that the world they knew has, in a short period of time, become a very different place. Some who once had a very secure future may now be in a place of great vulnerability. Many who were in employment that seemed protected and was fulfilling may now be at the end of a queue, relying on social welfare benefits. Others who dreamed of moving elsewhere to find work and happiness now realise that such places may no longer exist, as all countries experience the pain of economic turmoil. It seems that all the sacred cows are falling down, and that those things which once offered security and hope are gradually disintegrating.

No institution has been spared. Money, power and status are no longer offering the dream they once seemed to, but instead have brought much stress, anxiety and un-happiness. There is a growing awareness that our world is in a state of great flux and in need of much healing. Many are suffering as a consequence of the decisions and actions of others. People are very uncertain about where to look for leadership and guidance. There are deep wounds within society that need to be cleansed. But hope endures, even in the darkest of places. And it is only with hope that the possibility for change unfolds.

Change can, and will, happen when we are prepared to make choices that can seriously affect our own lives and the lives of those around us. We need to connect with the deepest part of ourselves. This is the place where I believe God dwells. This is the place that the outside world has forgotten or deliberately ignored. This is the place that holds the key to our transformation, and is the secret of our hope. We have made progress at so many levels in life today, but in other ways we still have a great deal to learn. There is much restlessness amongst us. There is much loneliness. There is much pain. But such longing can also become the threshold of new beginnings, where we can discover the creative force within.

When we begin to see ourselves and to accept ourselves as we are, when we see our world in all its brokenness, but also for its beauty and its potential to become a more beautiful place, then we have the power to begin to change. God is present in all things, in all people, but many have never had a profound experience of Him, or know who or what God is.

In my own life, I have had to begin a conversation with God. Such conversing will continue throughout my life. What I have learned is that, if I don't make time for this conversation, then I am hindering my relationship with God and it will cease to develop. But when I do make the time, I have learned that God will continue to reveal Himself in unexpected ways and experiences, and that He is immensely generous and always faithful. Each day allows us many possibilities. Tomorrow I cannot regain the time lost today.

God is always present, but I must be attentive to the moment. Being attentive means that I have to learn to listen. To listen, I have to be still within myself and have an awareness of all that is going on. Somewhere and at some time, I have to begin. There is always the *first* time.

This is a book of prayers, songs and reflections that I use in my various conversations with God. It has taken some time to write, as sometimes it is difficult to express in language the experience of God's loving presence. Many people think that they do not know how to pray, or that they should adhere to a certain formula. Many others believe that God would never listen to their prayers. Nothing is further from the truth. One of the most humbling experiences is to see someone on their knees, or sitting with open hands in prayer, enjoying the privilege of God visiting their lives.

Just to be present to God is prayer. I knew a very wise spiritual director who used to remind me that prayer was essentially 'wasting time with God'. There are many times when I have experienced the blessing of God's presence and felt close to Him. There are also times when I go through very dry periods and find prayer challenging, but I believe that every prayer is heard, no matter how small or how difficult to express.

When I pray, I also reconnect with the wider world, in recognition of the countless others created by the same God. Thus my relationship with God leads me into a relationship with others. This is how compassion is born. For when I am mindful of how we all share the earth, I become mindful of our common destiny. In doing so, I become aware of the sufferings of those who struggle; the pain of those who are hungry; the cry of those who are tortured; the tears of those who are lonely. Compassion also delights in the joy of others. I am happy when others are fortunate and blessed, for I share a common dream for the good of humanity.

In time, my prayer can lead me into action, when I am compelled to reach out. Compassion is an invitation to move beyond my own comfortable place, to the places of pain and emptiness of others – when I recognise that God is present in other broken lives.

Reaching out is not always easy and there is risk involved. What if the one to whom you reach out doesn't respond? What if I suffer rejection or humiliation? If compassion is rooted in prayer, then I hand over the situation to a higher power – to God. What is asked of me then is that I simply trust, and invite God into the situation. When you pray with compassion, you can penetrate the deeper meaning of God's presence in the world around us.

One of the things that I am trying to learn is how to become more aware of God's presence on so many levels around me. The author of the Psalms writes about the 'hiding place' of God. My experience has been that God hides Himself in many places, most notably within the human heart and, when we least expect it, He will reveal part of His beautiful image.

In introducing these prayers and songs, I have decided to include some writings from a diary that I kept while travelling in northern Sweden at the height of summer, 2007. I had been travelling on a hectic schedule. Through a kind invitation from a fellow musician, I was afforded time in a small lakeside village. It was one of the most beautiful places that I have ever visited and a hiding place for God:

It's almost night and I have been travelling for hours. The pale blue twilight hangs translucently overhead, as I travel further and further into the Swedish dusk. Gone is the incessant din and disturbance of airports and noisy traffic, and before me stretches the open sky with stars like veiled diamonds peering here and there: signposts for the weary traveller. Through the half-light, I can still see the red-stained wooden cabins nestling at the forest edge. Beneath a door a faint light emerges, casting shadows on the dewed reeds swaying in the night breeze.

After hours of driving, I reach my destination. I cannot sleep, so I go and sit by the side of the lake that skirts the village. It is profoundly beautiful. Just above the water, a gentle mist is rising like a silver gauze kissing the water's edge. It moves eerily, without effort. A rowing boat drifts slowly in ghost-like emptiness. Nearby, the white-washed church sends its steeple high into the night sky, reaching for the heavens while its shadow leans across the lake. It is a moment of rare beauty.

Up to this point, my life had been a deluge of clutter, with constant travelling, meeting deadlines, pastoral ministry, performances and concerts and, of course, trying to deal with my own inadequacies and weaknesses.

So often I have been searching for stillness, but am always tormented by anxiety, carrying the worries of the world on my shoulders. It's always easy to find something else to do. It can be much more difficult to stop and reflect. Here, I was being given a beautiful opportunity to be vigilant to myself and listen to my inner voice. This inner voice is the voice of God, and my communication with God is prayer.

To find stillness is not easy, as to find stillness one must also find silence. One is necessary for the other, I believe, but both are also difficult to sustain. Silence can be frightening and almost threatening, for when we journey into it, we can be left feeling very vulnerable. We are so used to noise, to the constant stream of other sounds, that to be alone with nothing can be ominous:

Here in the dusk light, I hear nothing at all except the call of a wild bird, whose shrill voice disturbs the peace of the evening. It is the lonely sound of a bird and seems to mirror the sound of my own soul crying out for direction.

It's interesting that in life today, silence is seen as a disturbance. Even in recreation time, people find silence very difficult and constantly need to listen to something or someone else. We are thus left feeling very exposed when everything stops and we are faced with simple silence.

It is only when we do stop and move into the silence that we can become aware of what is happening internally for us. Silence puts us in touch with all the chaos within. We begin to see the knots of entanglement that so often confuse and limit our lives. In silence we begin to hear all kinds of voices, even those that scream at us, sometimes at a deafening pitch because of unresolved tensions of one kind or another. These voices can sometimes render us powerless. So often in my own life I have heard the voices of blame and guilt, and unfinished work, shouting loudly within, and so disturbing my peace. It can be much easier to switch back on the iPod to drown out the confusing noise, but to there by the water's edge I simply sat and listened both to what was going on around me, and also within me.

To come into the stillness will mean a certain amount of detachment: leaving all behind for the sake of finding some inner contentment. But not abandoning all. Sitting by the lake, I experienced calm and serenity, even though I still needed to detach from so much going on inside my mind:

Slowly, very slowly, I learn just to sit with all. I acknowledge all and sit in the stillness. I find a sense of peace that had been missing in my life for so long. Now I am ready to converse with the One who is present. I do not feel trapped any longer by the incessant noise and distractions that constantly pervade my mind but rather, in acknowledging all, I am able to accept them and move on to a deeper place of calm and rest. I begin to have a greater sense of my own place in the scheme of things and I can acknowledge my strengths but also my weaknesses. This is the place and time when I can be self-effacing and honest before God who is present. This is the moment

*when I begin to learn to trust. This is
the moment of prayer.*

*I realise that I want to know more
and more of this God who creates so
beautifully. This is the essence of prayer:
to seek out the company of God.*

What many of us don't realise is that God
is already there, waiting for us. The time of
silence is God's gift to us. It is prompted by
His invitation. He longs to fill our lives with
His presence, but we are so suspicious of
others who want to give to us, for fear of
having to repay, that we are slow to accept
the graciousness of God. We live in a world
where we desperately want to control our
own destinies, so trusting in God, in
someone else, can seem very threatening.
But when we allow God to give to us, we
cannot but return for more and, in time, we
begin to learn how to trust.

Trust is not easy and comes at a cost. So
often we can hear people say: 'I trusted in
God before, but look what happened', or, 'I
asked God to help me, but see how I was
answered'. To hand over control to God

means we lose our independence, but if we only knew how much God wants to be close to us, accept us and care for us, then we might be able to realise that all He wants for us is completely for our good. So often in my own life when, with great difficulty, all I could do was let go and hand over all to God, I realised that He answered in the way that was best for me and in the situation, though I may not have realised it at that precise moment.

I remember travelling to Cyprus, where a young family member had become seriously ill while on vacation with her family. Thankfully, she is now doing well, but it was a time of great stress and fear. Not far from the hospital was a small Greek Orthodox Chapel, and in the midst of the mayhem of hospital life and the anxiety and fear for my niece, I often slipped into this quiet place to calm my worried heart. I never felt alone, and as I placed myself before the icon of the compassionate Christ, I was deeply aware that my words were heard. All I could do was trust that God would listen and answer in His own time and in His own loving way.

And He did. God shows compassion and love for us in so many different ways, even when we are not aware, and even when we think that all is lost. God is still there.

Of course the question that constantly arises is: how do we hear God speaking to us and how do we know what He is really saying? Because of the sort of world we live in, we like everything to be empirical and clear. But God's voice is different. He communicates in a more mysterious, subtle way. His voice is like a deep yearning in us, a voice we can hear deeply but cannot tangibly perceive. It is almost like hearing a dream. We awake with an awareness that can be difficult to describe. When God speaks to us, it will not be in an audible voice. It will happen at a much deeper level. He will call out to us through experiences, events, different circumstances. Modern life is lived at a very superficial level, where much attention is focused on image, and so it can be very difficult to 'hear' someone who communicates in silence.

A while ago I spent some time in Africa. One day, while travelling through the arid lands of the Turkana desert, we stopped in a Sudanese refugee camp. It was my impression of hell. So many thousands of people, crammed into a small area without proper facilities and services. So many different groups of people together, with little or no control over their daily lives, hungry and existing in terrible deprivation. As we drove into the heart of the camp, I was both frightened and saddened. I had never before witnessed such inhuman conditions, and realised that I had taken so much in life for granted.

The Land Rover that had transported us eventually stopped at the end of the camp, and we went to visit a Catholic priest who was one of the few non-nationals there. Meeting him was to have a profound effect on me. Father James had already spent two years in prison in Sudan with his people. Although Indian by birth, his life had been spent serving the people of Sudan. He radiated a sense of peace and serenity. I asked him if he was afraid, and he simply smiled. His complete trust in the providence of God did not leave room for fear nor judgement. Before we left, Father James took us into his chapel and as we sat there, he was completely calm, in stillness. I asked him for his blessing and in his humility he Fasked for mine in return. I had just met a man who was a holy man – a man of God. All around him there was chaos and mayhem, but he was the essence of serenity, having left his life and providence to the God he served and so profoundly believed in. I often think of this man.

When we come to sit with God in prayer, when we spend time developing a relation-ship with Him, our vulnerability is over-shadowed by His loving presence. We begin to free ourselves from the stones that weigh our hearts. The haunted places of our lives can be healed and the light of hope and promise can enter, however faintly it will begin. And if God is goodness, if God is gentleness, then slowly we too can become the same as Him.

Meister Eckhart, the great medieval mystic, said: 'You may call God love, you may call God goodness, but the best name for God is compassion.' Compassion is the language of Jesus, the Son of God. It was His way of life: when He encountered the pain and anguish of others, He reached out to their suffering. He healed the sick, He fed the hungry, He went into the places of decay and suffering and offered hope. His prayers became words in action, as He lived out His compassion. Mother Teresa of Calcutta once said: 'Never let anyone leave you without being happier. Be the living reflection of the goodness of God: gentleness in your eyes, gentleness in your smile.' This is prayer in action.

Jesus Himself called His followers into the places of silence and quiet. We read how He would go to a lonely place, by the lakeside or into the mountains, to pray. He recognised that to be alone with God, one needed to be alone with one's self. To commune with God is to be in the stillness, free from the distractions of all that erodes our sense of peace. When we pray, we visit the place where God dwells. Prayer is the door to the Divine longing in all of us. It is the threshold between heaven and earth, between the Divine and the human.

There is something very natural in acknowledging the presence of God when in a beautiful place. Our forefathers had a great appreciation for the presence of God in the natural world around us, which was reflected in their language and spiritual rituals. Their physical world was imbued with a sense of God's presence. In Sweden, I experienced the same sence:

Now I begin to pray. I open my hands and feel the light breeze blowing through my fingers. I am conscious of the line from Psalm 46: 'Be still and know that I am God.'

I hear the water quietly lapping against the rowing boat. The gentle waves beat rhythmically against the wood, almost in time with the rhythm of my own breathing. With each breath, I inhale the mystery of the moment and exhale the stress and anxiety of the day. The silence begins to reveal a hidden world, as I become aware of so many blessings. It is getting darker, but the Northern Lights are becoming brighter. I add my own words to the millions of words and thoughts communicated in prayer this night. I add my silence to the silence of hearts beating the world over.

I understand what it is to be intimate with God, in this sacred space where He becomes teacher, lover, healer, reconciler and listener. This is where I can be most honest: without mask, without fear. The God who created the sun, the God who flung the stars into the night sky, the God who tosses the great waves in stormy waters, the God who was humbly born in Bethlehem, now comes to dwell in my heart in these moments of prayer. I am reminded that every thought I have, every word I utter, is already known by God.

The wild bird has circled the lake and veers westward to her nesting place. Now the mist is rising off the water, cocooning the old rowboat. The light has gone from beneath the red wooden chalet door, and the church spire fades into the shadows of the evening light. Soon the dawn light will emerge from behind the forest and the stars will hide themselves in Paradise. In these moments of prayer, Heaven opens a window to shine on the soul, lighting the darkened places of pain and tears, and blessing the sacred spaces of our living. As the mist rises and rests on the sleeping lake, so too will my prayer rise and find shelter, for tomorrow God will come to visit again.

There is a lakeside within the heart of all of us where we can go at any time. There is an empty boat waiting to take you to the far shore of stillness, beyond the mists of your anxiety. Let the calm waters nurture your weary soul and may you hear the gentle voice of God's compassion welcome you home. May you discover the hope that lies not on distant shores, but at the very heart of your own soul.

THE LIGHT OF DAY

I have never woken to the same sky. Each morning has a new horizon. Each sky appears as never before. One day, the canvas is a swirling mass of blue-grey cloud and the next, I am visited by a canopy of white cumulus clouds with shafts of pale yellow beams highlighting the foothills, as seen from my window on an early spring morning.

The Divine Artist wants to set each new day against a background of His choosing, so that I can experience His infinite creativity and beauty. In ancient Celtic times, there was a great reverence for the awakening of another day. Putting on one's clothes was akin to robing oneself in the dignity of the new day, clothing the soul in grace. The light of each new day was an invitation to immerse oneself in fresh possibilities, where change and challenge walked hand in hand. Such people believed they were never alone. Every action was ritualised, in the belief that God the Divine Creator watched over every moment with deep love and respect for the human condition. Each day becomes a time and place of new possibilities, a threshold of transformation.

We never know what will unfold before us. Change can be slow, and sometimes frightening. To go where we have never been before demands courage and conviction. There is a whole world waiting to be discovered, but perhaps we have become so dimmed by the limitations of modern living that we need to rediscover the consciousness of God in our own time, in our own lives. We have re-fashioned the world in our own images, hence our world is filled with greed, hate and unhappiness. If we could reassess our position and become 'God conscious', then we might begin to realise that this life is the gift of God to us. To believe this brings a new awareness, and subsequently a new freedom. As soon as I embrace the concept of God, He is joined to me: to my heart, to my soul. All things become providential and life is imbued with meaning. It is hard to surrender everything at once, but God is a patient God and will wait a lifetime for our response.

To be 'God conscious' is to see with the eyes of God, to think with the mind of God, to speak with the voice of God and to love with the heart of God. Then, you begin to experience the world through the heart of the Creator. Every waking day holds many grace-filled opportunities. The grey-black sky can in time turn to azure blue, but all in God's time. When I allow God to become part of my life, His giving is endless. The God of surprises is forever engaging. When God visits our lives, we kiss the dark adieu, and we gently encounter the light of day.

PRAYER FOR HOPE

L ord

When a darkened sky surrounds me
And sets upon my life
And the greying mist still lingers
And haunts the coming night
Let me find hope

When the cry of hurts and sorrows
Still echo in my heart
And I cannot face the evening
And tomorrow is too far
Let me find hope

Let me find hope
In different form and guise
In the warm embrace of lovers
In a sign from listening eyes
In the silence of a stranger who utters
    not a word
But comes to walk beside me
And heart to heart reverbs

Let me find hope
In the trusting of a child
In the silent pride of parents
Or the rest of those retired
In hands that lift the weary
In fingers bent in prayer
Signs of resurrection
Devoid of all despair

Let me find hope
In the smallest simple ways
In the changing of the seasons
In the birthing in the clay
In dew that cleanses morning
In dusk that calms the day

Let me find hope
When children sleep contented
Far from fear and dread
And peace is no illusion
But spins a silver thread
Where You are waiting
Not far from Heaven's edge

Let me find hope
Before my soul departs
Faith, hope and love –
Your gift
To every hopeful heart.

PRAYER FOR INSPIRATION

Lord

There are the days when
I long for inspiration
To move beyond the boundaries of
    banality
To search for a deeper meaning in my life

May I be inspired by all that surrounds me
All that feeds my senses and my soul
Your touch on humanity
In nature's garden
The wind that brushes my hair
The sun that kisses my face
The life-giving air

May the well-springs of goodness
In every human heart
Draw such reserves from my own hidden
    depths

May simplicity inspire me to be humble
May kindness inspire me to be generous
May forgiveness inspire me to compassion
May misery inspire me to justice

Let the pain of our world
Inspire me to seek wholeness and healing
For the hungry
For the lonely
For the frightened
For the old ones
For the new born
May Your beauty Lord
That is boundless
Stir my heart to offer more

May I see in the stars
In all colours
In all life
In all forms of artistic expression
In beautiful notes that soothe the soul
In poets, words that find their home
    in searching hearts
Your haunting presence

May I be inspired by the genius of each
   person
Unique
Graced with Divine beauty
Capable of boundless possibility
Known to some
Forever hidden to others

May Your touch upon my life
Draw others to be inspired
By my own self giving
However small   ,

For when I look to You I
Am inspired
What need I more but
This desire
Your touch upon my life.

PRAYER FOR THE NEW MORNING

Lord

When the silver night surrenders to the sun
When stars will fade as morning light will
    come
So too may Your blessing fall upon this
    day

When the night of sleep has cast its quilt
    away
And life is stirred, embracing new the
    day
So too may Your peace come fall upon
    our way

Bless this day
With light
With love
With peace
With justice
With integrity

Bless our children
Bless our aged
Bless all people
Who pass our way

May we touch with Your grace
All places in need of compassion
All places of hunger
All places where hearts are hurting
Fearful of this new day

May we never fail to see
Your dignity in every soul
May we give as we receive
All that life unfolds

May our hearts give shelter
To lost and lonely spirits
Who need a place of rest
Without fear of judgement
In the peace of Heaven's breath
Drawn from this new day.

PRAYER OF THE ARTIST

Lord

I do not have the mind of Michelangelo
Nor can I mix the rusts of Rembrandt's
    hues
But in these scripted words, O God
I place my trust in You

You are the Divine Craftsman
You create in whirls and geometrical swirls
Your canvas in unending change
The orchid's face will bear Your name

Magenta, red and cobalt blue
The life-blood touch in all You do
Inspire O Lord my heart anew

You wash the amber sky
You paint the harvest moon
In semblance rich and rare
You dress the winter noon

Wash my soul with the pure water of Your
    Divine imagination
Cleanse my mind that I might see Your
    world as You
Take my hand and guide each stroke with
    humble poise
Remove my pride and ego too

Let me illumine the true image of Your
    beauty
Let me draw from the well-springs of
    silence
Let sweet solitude embrace my palette and
    my paint

May I uncover Your many hidden faces
May I heal the hearts that long for colour
    in grey lives
May I reach beyond banality
And bring the shadows into light

May I never take for granted
The gift that I employ
Within my heart's safe-keeping
No self-doubt to destroy

May this inner eye forever hold
My kind Creator's gaze
In every charcoal portrait see
Your kindly face arrayed

So bless us Lord
That we might know
Your grace in every soul
To reach beyond
All time and space
As once did
Michelangelo.

PRAYER OF THE FISHERMAN

Lord

As we put out into the deep
We place ourselves into Your keep

All that lies before us
Your grandeur
O blue-grey wave and water
Your sacred work of art

Every fish that swims
Every lurking shell
Every coral of beauty
Beneath the surf and swell
Bears the imprint of Your name

May this boat
Rise with the ebb and flow of each tide
And glide
To the rhythm
Of Your heart

May no storm
Separate us from
Sheltering coves
May we never lose hope
In Your eternal presence

Calm the seas
With Your gentle breeze
May dolphins dance
And seagulls swoop
To a rich harvest

May we see again
The miracle of full nets
As we too cast
Out to starboard
As once You told
Your fishermen

May the night come calmly
Guiding us to a safe harbour
Where every lighthouse
Reaches the hidden depths of Your
    presence
Lighting the darkness of distant lives

Lord take to Your Self
All who lie in the sleep of the sea
All souls lost in service
May love still shed a tear

And when the sun is setting
In gold across the bay
In You we find our anchor
In You we rest and pray

Come walk across the water
Come lead us through the dark
O fisherman of Galilee
Come be our morning star.

PRAYER OF
THE GARDENER

Lord

The Magnolia tree is opening
To the scent of the apple blossom
The wildflowers dance in the breeze
Your gift O God for all to see

When I hold the wet soil in my hands
I hold the wonder of Your Being
You create from the dust
Life in abundance

Your creation is constant
Your love made visible to all
In every waking hour
In every tiny flower
In every living cell

Bless the labours of my work
With patience
With perseverance
That in the changing seasons

I might see
Your Divine imagination
Unfolding

May I bless the soul of my mother earth
May I respect her goodness
May I treat her kindly

May every flower and every tree
Remind me often
That Paradise was made for me
For all

Lord may I
Replenish
Restore
Renew
All that I receive from You

May Your gentle rain
Falling on dry and arid ground
Cleanse and refresh
The parched earth
Washing the green land
And my eyes
To watch in wonder

May the morning sun
Rise with rays from
Your warm heart O God
Healing our earth
Bringing to birth
Seed and sapling

May these chiselled hands
Worn with life's lines
Plant
Sow
Reap and grow
O God

May the dews of grace
Fall silently each night
Your warm and silver light
From the gentle moon
Casting shadows of calm
On life's garden.

PRAYER OF THE MUSICIAN

Lord

The whole universe is a song
From which You have created
Beautiful sounds
Eternal echoes
Resounding
Resonating
Replenishing
Music to wash our souls
To heal the hunger of our hearts

You are the Divine Musician
Conducting Your Symphony of Life
Each note on each page
Continues day after day
Age to age

You channel Your gift
Through frail minds
And gentle fingers
Symphony

Concerto
Ballad
The wonders of Your making

Drawing tears
Awakening hearts
Calming spirits
And through the human voice
You reach countless others
Drawing us into another world

Help us to appreciate Your Divine gift
Opening our lives to Your eternal presence
May we not squander what You offer
Nor deaden our lives to the beauty of
Your sound

May we be inspired constantly
Drawing songs from stones
Discovering worlds unknown
Melodies the heart is yet to hear

May we learn the beauty of silence
The sister of sound
The birthplace where all songs are born
May quiet song surround us

When we are wounded and weary
When life is decaying and dreary
When stones hide our hearts

May we hear the rhythm of Your dance
Beating in every heart
Celebrating life
Communing with the whole cosmos
All that lies before us
Your festive chorus

When we sit in silence
May we hear new notes that echo
Through the corridors of time
In melody and rhyme
From other songs of other days

Ever ancient ever new
May we write anew
A song of love for You.

PRAYER TO
CELEBRATE LIFE

Lord

Open my eyes
And see the amazing world You have
    created
In the hundreds of thousands of stars
You have found a place for me

You have blessed my life
With wisdom
With imagination
With spirit

You constantly write love letters to me
In Your creation
Your fingerprints upon every particle

Each drop of rain contains Your world
What colour the kingfisher carries
The wildflowers bow in the breeze
All tides and seas
Know the song of Your creation

Evening light that fades
Bringing night in dewy haze
Your gift O God
Our time of contemplation

Lord
May we mirror Your beauty
For we are made for You
We complete Your Universe

May all we do
May all we think
Be a song of joy

May we add our voices
To the song of monks
In the quiet hours of night
Who wait patiently for the dawn

May we never grow weary
Of mystery
Of beauty
Of searching
For restless is the heart
Until we find our home in You
And with You
And with ourselves

For in You we move
And have Your being
Yet no ear has heard
Nor eye has seen
What You have prepared
For those
Who want to love
You.

I had the great privilege of travelling in Africa and experienced the heartache of poverty and hunger but also the hopes and dreams of an amazing and resilient people. The generosity of many who spent their lives in service of others gave birth to the new light each day and inspired this song.

BELIEVE

I will sing you a different song
Echoes that go on and on
I will dance to a different beat
Guided by my head and feet
I will play you a different tune
Voices that will call to you
Whispers that you hear all round
Whispers of a different sound

Believe – what I tell you is true
Believe – that this song is for you
Believe – in your heart some things pass
Believe – there is love that can last

I will sing of a different world
Somewhere a new voice is heard
I will dream of a different place
No tears from a frightened face
I will sing of a question too
A question that is just for you
Will you, will you take the chance
To follow in a different dance?

Refrain

*This song is based on the writings of
Mother Teresa of Calcutta, whom I had
the honour of meeting a number of times.
When we reach out to those who are
wounded and without love, what we
receive in return is far beyond what we
imagine. To offer hope to another is the
real gift of love.*

FAR BEYOND

Far beyond all dreaming
Far beyond the place of despair
Far beyond believing
You will find His love if you dare
Far beyond riches that fade
Far beyond this very day

I am thirsting, I am blind
I am stumbling, hear my cry
I am lonely, filled with fear
I am thirsting, I am thirsting
Who will quench this thirst for me?

I am silent, world alone
I am orphaned without a home
I am no one, can this be?
I am weeping, I am weeping
Who will dry my tears for me?

I am brother, I am son
I am family, I am one
I am stranger, should this be?
I am pleading, I am pleading
Who will hear my cries for me?

*Originally written in the Irish language,
this song speaks of the many hiding places
of God. We can discover God's Divine
presence when we dare to journey
into the silence*

ḦIDING PLACE

I *will search in the silence*
For Your hiding place
In the quiet Lord
I seek Your face.

Where can I discover
The well-springs of Your love?
Is my searching and seeking in vain?
How can I recover the beauty of Your
    word?
In the silence I call out Your name

Refrain

Where can I find shelter
To shield me from the storm?
To find comfort though dark be the night?
For I know my welfare is ever in Your
    sight
In the shadows I long for Your light

Refrain

Lead me in Your footsteps
Along Your ancient way
Let me walk in the love of the Lord
Your wisdom is my heart's wealth
A blessing all our days
In the silence I long for Your word.

Refrain

THE LIGHT OF HOME

No matter where we travel, we will always long for home. It is the place where the heart is most at peace and where we should feel most secure. It is where love is nurtured, where we receive our moral compass and learn to take our place in the wider world. When I am travelling late at night, I often wonder at the stories behind the light of each door. There is no home without its joys and sorrows, without its heartbreak and blessings, and yet it is the place to which we will continue to return as long as there is a light in the window, or an open door.

To the people of the Celtic world, God not only dwelt in the local church, but the family home was His resting place, the focus of His longing to visit the hearts that were open to Him. Every home in that era contained a hearth: the centre of each house where people gathered for warmth, food and camaraderie. The fire was a reminder for each person that they too needed renewal and replenishment. Beautiful rituals took place around the home, wherein God and all of Heaven were invoked and welcomed for protection and blessing. The lighting or the kindling of the fire in the morning by the woman of the household was accompanied by a quiet prayer, that the fire would bring the light of Heaven to those living there and all who would gaze on its bright flames throughout that day and night. The miracle of fire was a gift of Divine providence.

In a world devoid of all modern conveniences, people knew the gift of true hospitality. To welcome a neighbour or indeed a stranger was to welcome a blessing from Heaven. Perhaps the real wisdom of such times was the natural acceptance of the omnipresence of God, who becomes very real when He is invoked as such into the ordinariness of the daily living. From birth to death, from the kindling to the quelling of the fire, to the daily conversations that began and ended with a Divine invocation, God was as naturally present in this world as the warm winds and soft rain that fell upon the green earth.

Today, home can mean something very different and yet it is the setting that we are drawn towards when we need security and connection. It is often said that when a mother dies, the heart of the home is missing. This is because of the ability of a mother to exude love. Such love will always infuse our sense of belonging. We all need to belong, and when we find a place where our deepest needs are met and our deepest sentiments can be shared, we experience the blessing of home. That is not to say that pain, hurt and betrayal cannot also be found in the safest of places and often when some look back at their home, they do so with pain and loss and are in need of healing from such experiences.

When we leave our home and take a new road on life's journey, what will sustain us is the love that we have experienced among those who are closest to us. So often, our new home will be modelled on aspects of our first home, though we will also give it our own instinctive marks. When we speak of home, we are internally drawn to the first cradle of our existence. An internal light will continue to draw us to the place where we once were held in secure and loving arms.

Though my father left his boyhood home many years ago to settle in the midlands of Ireland, I still remember as a young boy us driving through the country roads on an August evening to his childhood home by the sea on the south Irish coast. Every winding road and every whitewashed wall drew my father closer to the home which he had left many years previously, but which had never left him. On such journeys, I longed to open a window to his mind, as I have no doubt that it was blessed with cherished memories of being a young boy, running through the fields of golden barley to play the ancient game of hurling in neighbouring fields, until the evening sun surrendered to the harvest moon and it was time to seek the light of home.

PRAYER FOR GRANDPARENTS

L ord

We are privileged to know
The blessing of grandparents

To know
The knowledge of years
The wisdom of fears
The gift of tears

To know the warm embrace
The kindly face
The unjudging space
The listening place

Lord
May we follow
In footsteps
That honour the mystery of their giving
The sacrifices of their living
Their gracious forgiving

May they find in us
Warm compassion
And endless passion
For life and love

May we move to the gentle rhythm of their
    living
May we cherish them with empathy and
    patient giving

May we know the sacredness of faith
Blessed by their constant believing
In You Lord
In life
In love
In trust
In truth

May they be free from
Anxiety
Pain and sorrow

May they find in each other
A faithful companion
Where silence is the bridge
To blessed memories of

Other times and other days
May they never be lonely
Because we are too busy
May our words of gratitude and thanks
Never be empty
May the fruits of their lives
Ripen into a harvest of plenty

May they find joy
In their children's children
In the company of loved ones
In the warm embrace of old friends
In the knowledge that Your promise
Never ends

Lord bless them
All the days of their lives.

PRAYER FOR
GROWING OLD

Lord

So soon the years creep up
So soon the rings of the tree collect
So soon the chapters of life are filled

The harvest time is here
And we gather into barns of memory
Blessings in abundance

How sweet is the recall
Of days and nights
When the moon was always silver
The peat fires coloured gold
When we danced through fields 'til
    morning
Never dreamed of growing old

And You were there
At every passing stage
The birthing and the dying
You coloured every page

With Your ever-silent presence
We knew You when You called
When hearts were kissed by sorrow
When pride had known a fall

You were there
You were there

In the freedom of these years
May we unlatch the window of all stored
    dreams
Healing the spaces and places
Where love was missing
And we sometimes closed the door
Never realising
There was always more and more
To learn

Now we have time to savour
To gather and to sow
Reflecting on life's wisdom
Watch the wildflowers grow

And You have been so faithful
A light throughout the years
Restoring fallen dignity

Catching falling tears
Time has found us gentle
In silence we can pray
Be with us Lord
Our comfort
At the closing of the day.

PRAYER FOR STUDENTS

Lord

Why is it that at the most confusing time
    of our lives
We have to learn the most?
We have to carry so much within
We must learn to listen
We must listen to learn

All is decision
All is choice
All is question

Help me to find friends
Who will accept me
Help me to be strong
When difficult choices come
Help me to live with values that You value

When I am anxious
When I am hurting
When I am confused
When I am lazy

When I am troubled
When I am fearful
When I am rejected
When I am ridiculed
When I am moody
When I am misunderstood

Be with me Lord

When I am happy
When I celebrate
When I win
When I fall in love
When I pass with flying colours
When I finish my assignment
When I find my place
When I belong

Be with me Lord

Teach me understanding
Teach me compassion
Teach me empathy
Teach me respect
Teach me graciousness
Teach me forgiveness

Teach me courage
That others will find in me
What I long to be

On each new day
Bless those who love me
Bless those who teach me
Bless those who befriend me
Bless those who accept me

Bless my family and friends
All who know me

May all that I have learned
Be not in vain
For if I have never lost
I will not search again.

PRAYER OF A FATHER

Lord

As I look upon my own father
You now have given me the privilege
Of my own family

Help me to accept with humility
This sacred gift

May I be gentle and strong
Knowing right from wrong
May I be firm yet fair

May my wife find in me
A companion for life
A true friend
A kind listener
May my children know
Protection
Affection
Direction

May I open for them
The book of knowledge
The secret doorway to adventure
May the child in me always accompany the
    child in them

May I hold them in times of fear
May I dry the eyes that cry soft tears
May we journey together through many
    years

Lord may they know You
Because of me
Your consoling compassionate way
Woven through life each day

May I be silent when I need to hear
Affirm
And gently steer
The anxious heart to a place of calm

Lord may I be blessed in my children's
    children
May my wonder never cease
May I find with self-acceptance
The gift of inner peace

May I rest with quiet contentment
And make this silent prayer
Father of all Fathers
Guide our earthly way.

MOTHER'S PRAYER

Lord

I have counted each day waiting
I have whispered new names each night
I have held this child for ever

I have dreamed dreams
Beyond my imagining
That come to life in the
Tiny fingers that wind around my thumb

Whatever this child is
And will become
May he know the wisdom of Your Temple
    days
May he lift the wounded with Your
healing way
May his heart be humble should he stray

When Your mother let You go
Did she walk the dusty roads forever in her
    heart
Following You with love

Or did she learn to trust
Even when You walked *that* hill
And spread Your arms
For me
And all humanity?

Help me place my life, my flesh, my child
Into Your care, Your arms
Mind him for me
Mind him well

Then one day Lord
He can tell his child
Of You and of love
As well.

PRAYER OF A NEWLY MARRIED COUPLE

Lord

At last this day of days has come
We have been preparing
For days and years
This is the day of dreams

Thank You Lord
For the meeting of
Our hearts
Our lives
Our souls
All is yearning
All is hope

Come bless our lives
You who see into future ways
With Your eternal wisdom
Protect our nights and days

Make our home
A place of joy
When storm clouds gather
Let no hurt destroy

May Your angels
Find a home from Heaven
Therein
When days are sad
May we hear them sing

Bless us with children
Fulfilling our dream
Placed in Your trusting
Our future unseen

May friends young and old
Cross this threshold to find
A sacred embrace
A welcome in kind

Lord of Love
May we know
The gift of Your Spirit
In times of strength
In times of sorrow

When hearts are strong
When hearts are hollow
Whisper courage to the wind

May the harvest of our lives
Mellow our hearts
Where silence is sacred
And words can depart
For You are there
Keeping watch
In our twilight years

This day is but the beginning
Of love in eternity
Beyond
Above
Below
How could we ever know
The depth of Your love

Till death do us part . . .
What is death
Only finding love
Beyond the stars.

PRAYER OF THE WORKER

Lord

I rise in the dark of moon time
Another day is birthing
I am grateful for work
I am grateful for opportunity when so
    many so are without

Bless my work in this day
My world
My mind
My hands
My heart

Create in me
Through me
With me
For me

May my hands be Your hands
May my eyes be Your eyes

May my mind be Your mind
May Your sacred touch
Bless all that I touch this day

All possibilities
All actions
All decisions
All failures
All conversation
All resting

Calm me Lord
In times of stress
In times of worry
In times of burden

When I am weary
When I am tired
When I am despondent
When I am anxious

At the end of the day
May I know the graciousness of words
Like 'thank you'
Placed upon my lips
May I know the humility

Of recognising others' good work
May I know fulfilment
In serving

Lord
And as this day departs
May sleep come
To all contented hearts.

PRAYER TO BE A
GOOD NEIGHBOUR

Lord

I thank You for
Friends and neighbours
All who bless my life
Each day quietly and humbly
May I always appreciate
Their kindly presence

May my eyes see the beauty
Of each heart and soul
May my ears listen to kind words
May I hear the call of those
Who cry out in need
May I hear Your voice
In theirs

May I speak only kind words
Without harsh judgement
May I encourage but keep silent
When others criticise

May my words be words of comfort
And praise
May I speak consoling words
When sorrow fills their days

May I have hands that reach out
To hold
To hug
To help
To open in loving acceptance

May I have feet that will hurry
To where help is needed
And every deed
Seeks no reward

May I have a heart
Where others can find refuge
Where empathy abounds
Where love is found
Through a door that's open wide

Lord if You would come
And be my neighbour
Make Your dwelling place in mine
That I might learn to be Your servant

Love's constant sign
And should there come a day
When hurt confounds us
Or pain surround's us
May we learn to forgive
And never part
With hurting hearts
But find the words where forgiveness lies

Lord bless each day
With wonder
Joy and health
That I might learn
To love my neighbour
As myself.

This song is about time. Nothing is as precious to us as time. As we grow older we begin to appreciate its preciousness, and how time passed can never be regained. One of the greatest gifts to give another is the gift of time.

EVER HAVE THE TIME

If I could count my blessings with my
    hands
If I could speak the words your heart
    would understand
If I could know the things that I should
    know
Is there something that love has left to
    show?
If I could read the wisdom of your mind
If I could search the heavens for a sign
If I could only treasure all that's mine
I wonder if I'll ever have the time

'Cause time will wait for no one in the end
Time goes on without you, on that you can
    depend
And though you may be wondering where
    it ends
You can save it, you can lose it
You can chase it, you can choose it
You can be its victim or its friend

If I could turn your darkness into day
If I could stop all beauty from decay
If I could be the person that you need
I should listen to your longings and take
    heed
If I could learn that time will never last
I should savour all the memories of the
    past
If I could only treasure all that's mine
I wonder if I'll ever have the time

In the end love outlasts all time
In the end love will never die.

There is a great need among us humans to belong. We need to know that we are loved and important to one another. This next song was inspired by the fact that we often find this love and acceptance in the most unexpected of places and times.

I FOUND LOVE

I found love in unsuspecting places
In tired and worn-out faces
I found love, so near and yet so far
I found hope when it was least expected
When the world would not protect it
I found love, for love hides in every heart

As our world is growing older
There are burdens on each shoulder
As we try to find the place where we
should be
When we waste away the time
We keep searching for the signs
Yet what we need is sometimes very near

Every day brings different news
Different voices, different views
And we highlight all the difference and the
    blame
Different colour, different creed
All are human, all have needs
And within us all – a heart that beats the
    same

I found love in unsuspecting places
In tired and worn-out faces
I found love, so near and yet so far
I found hope when it was least expected
When the world would not protect it
I found love, yes, love hides in every heart.

This song is written in admiration and thanks for grandparents, who have much to teach us. There is an old Japenese proverb that says: 'Happy the home where many generations live.'

IF I GAKE THE GIME

And if I take the time to thank the Lord
For all that You've done
In history and mystery, the blessings He
    has shown
And if I take the time to pray
For generations gone
May God reward you all your days
For all that you have done

And every generation
Will find the words to sing
And every generation
Will God's praises sing
So may we hold this legacy
In love to always last
May God be with us all our days
The future and the past

Refrain

And if I take the time to thank the Lord
To know the things you've done
The days and nights of sacrifice

The selflessness you've shown
You are the calm in stormy days
My comfort when alone
You are the Christlight in my heart
That always leads me home

Refrain

And if I take the time to thank the Lord
And say a prayer for you
To thank Him for the loving way
His love is found in you
And when He calls me to His side
I know you will be there
To guide me to a place of love
And eternity we'll share.

One of my favourite songs is imbued with images of nature. In Ireland the light is constantly changing as clouds affect our vision. Yet, beyond them, the light of the sun is ever-present. This metaphor of the Divine presence beyond the 'veil' is found in ancient texts.

THE CLOUDS' VEIL

Even though the rain hides the stars
Even though the mist swirls the hills
Even when the dark clouds veil the sky
You are by my side

Even when the sun shall fall in sleep
Even when at dawn the sky shall weep
Even in the night when storms shall rise
You are by my side, You are by my side

Bright the stars at night
That mirror Heaven's way to You
Bright the stars in light
Where dwell the saints in love and truth

Even when the sun shall fall in sleep
Even when at dawn the sky shall weep
Even in the night when storms shall rise
You are by my side, You are by my side

Held in memory
The thoughts we have of yesterday
May our future be
A resting place
Where love will stay.

THE LIGHT BEYOND
THE DARK

In ancient Ireland, there were certain times of the year that held great significance. One of the most important dates was that of the Winter Solstice: the shortest day of light in the whole year. In the prehistoric burial ground of Newgrange in central Ireland, the great engineers of Neolithic times ensured that the sun found its way through a narrow opening at the top of the burial mound and that, as the sun rose on the shortest day, shafts of light flowed down through the passage there, illuminating the burial chamber with light. At the moment this happened, the people of those times believed the souls of their dead would find their way to the next world. What a beautiful belief from a people who had not yet experienced the knowledge and truth of the Resurrection of Jesus; who were living at least three thousand years before He was born.

The month of December always held the shortest and darkest day, but once this had passed, one could look forward again to the longer hours of light that would eventually come. To reach the light, one had to pass through the darkest night.

Day and night come from the same source. They are part of creation. Yet human nature will always veer towards the light. With the light, we become aware of all that is beautiful. We learn to identify colour. Light gives names to the blue sky, or the green earth, or the golden sunset. Light draws us towards beauty, and transparency is her sister. It is hard to hide in the light.

In early Celtic times, there was a great reverence for light. Angels were thought of as coming from the place of light, the place where the most high God dwelled. When the earliest signs of light appeared in the morning sky, the people were attuned to the presence of God, blessing their day. They were also aware that the dark nights of storms could come when least expected, when the light of day would be over-shadowed by the black dark, but their trust in their kind Creator enabled these people to face the dark night and believe in the promise of a new dawn.

Darkness in its own way can also overpower the light of our world today. Suffering can suddenly visit our lives and we are haunted by fear and isolation. We feel abandoned by the light, as we find ourselves in a dark place of despair. Everyone, no matter who they are, will experience the pain of darkness at one time or another. Suffering knows no bounds and is not selective, even though at times we may feel that we are the only ones. Pain can appear in many guises. The body can be worn down by the daily grind of physical constraints and illness, or the mind may be haunted by painful memories that lead to profound suffering and require deep healing. Perhaps one of the saddest afflictions of modern living is that of loneliness. To feel cut off from human contact, to feel ignored or abandoned or to be rejected by another: all this can lead one into the darkness of despair.

Have you ever visited an empty house after its owners have moved out? Walking around the empty rooms, you hear nothing only the loud clamour of footsteps on stripped floors. Such a house can be haunted by memory, the sounds and sights of days now consigned to history. So too can a soul become empty when it loses contact with the very essence of who it is, and now lives in isolation, in a void of darkness. The soul will seek solace in all kinds of places, but ultimately will have to face its own darkness so that eventually healing can occur.

Why do we have to suffer? This question has been asked from time immemorial and there is no easy answer. In the Christian tradition, suffering is central to the life and death of Jesus Christ. He not only knew suffering, but embraced it. He knew the pain of the human condition. But Jesus was such a contradiction to those around Him. The great hatred and jealousy towards Him was met by tender compassion and a sincere forgiveness. Dying the way He did was reserved for the most hardened of criminals, yet He was still able to find words of forgiveness in His final moments, and He was also prepared to invite a criminal who was dying alongside Him, to accompany Him into Paradise.

But His story did not end there. The Cross on which He died, a symbol of great suffering and hatred, was lifted high on a hill for all to see. It was surrounded by the darkness of the human condition, but was soon transformed by the light of the Resurrection. When Jesus opened His arms on the Cross that day, He embraced the pain and weakness of generations to come – all the genocide, all ethnic cleansing, all abuse, all rejection, all hatred and all the weaknesses of the human condition were carried to present on the hill of Calvary in those terrible moments.

Can you imagine the pain of His mother Mary, who stood by watching, so numb and helpless? Then in her profound pieta moment, she held in her arms her beloved son, lifeless and dead. In that moment she embraced all our suffering, all our anguish, all our despair, to place all in the tomb with her beloved Jesus.

But, beyond the darkness of these terrible hours, the light comes. The Resurrection turns human life on its head. He who is dead has risen. We experience a new light, never before known to humankind. In the beautiful ritual of Easter night re-enacted for generations by Christians, we light the Easter Candle and hear the words: 'a light no darkness can extinguish'.

This is the light that reaches beyond all darkness; that guides all those who will struggle on the path of their own suffering; that brings hope to the hearts that have known nothing but fear, anxiety and worry. This is the light that reaches into prisons, that lights up lonely hostels, that warms winter hearts, that shelters grieving souls, gives courage to those who carry heavy burdens and guides weary travellers. This is the light that goes before us, the light we will follow. But we will not be alone: someone will accompany us, and wait for us on the other side.

We may be in a time of darkness now, but the dark night will not last. Soon will come the morning – the light beyond the dark.

PRAYER ON THE DEATH OF A LOVED ONE

Lord

My heart is numb
The one I love has died
And I have cried and cried

There is an empty space in my heart
That I long to fill

As You wept for Lazarus Your friend
Your human heart was breaking
So now I take Your place

Lift the veil that I might see beyond my
    grief
Where love is pure and
Light will reach beneath
These empty walls

May no harm come to them
Who have taken leave

Pilgrims of Paradise
May their journey be gentle
And blessed memory
Lighten their way

May they see the glimmer
Of Heaven's light
Calling them deeper and deeper
Into eternal beauty

May they recognise the kindly faces
Of loved ones, old friends and neighbours
Who have gathered to greet them
And take them to the land of eternal
    summer

May they see You Lord
As You are
In radiant beauty
With a gaze from beautiful eyes
That never leaves them
May they know the sweet embrace
Of Your soft tanned hands

Lord
In my empty moments
May blessed memory
Be the bridge
From my heart to Heaven

So rest in peace O gentle soul
Until that day
When love will call us home.

PRAYER FOR A BROKEN RELATIONSHIP

Lord

I never realised until now
That separation is so difficult
I have never been here before
Since love has closed the door

I have asked so many questions
All with useless gain
Theorised and analysed
The balance and the blame

What happened, Lord
Two people
On a road of discovery
Could we not listen
Could we not learn
Did life become so self-absorbed
We could not discern

Now I cry tears, Lord
For all that could

All that should
Have been

In this time of separation
And healing of the wound
I am haunted by a sadness
That fills the empty room

From the distance
I see what I've never seen before
The veil of rage is lifting
Sunlight skirts the floor

There is a kindness in every heart
So far and yet so near
In my finite indignation
I was blind and could not see

From the other side
There's a different view
Perhaps I don't have all the answers
Even if I think I do

Lord, into our hour of broken dreams
Bring Your healing
In the knowledge that

Our souls cannot live without love
And love cannot exist without
You

If love comes to dwell
In our hearts
Then so must You

For You
Are never unfaithful
You never grow old

In times of disillusion
We are never left alone

You are there, Lord
Yes, always there.

PRAYER FOR HEALING

Lord

Illness has come to me when I least expected
Coming to me without invitation
So swiftly that I had no time to prepare

But You knew, Lord

And You know me well
You know my fears
How much I worry
So much anxiety
I do not need to tell

What choice do I have
Shall I suffer with resigned indignation
Or have You allowed these moments
To bring me to a clearer destination?

Help me to befriend this illness
My silent companion
This intrusion
This invasion of my serenity and soul

Heal the deep darkness that surrounds me
Heal the fears that confound me
Bring bright beautiful moments of healing
    light
Through the closed shutters of my
    paralysis

Help these days to be
Not the end
But merely
The beginning
Of transformation in my life

Heal me Lord
All sources of pain
And infection
All self-loathing and rejection
May You bring ease my to dis-ease

Hold me during the deepest moments of
    despair
Place words on my lips
That become Your prayer

Help me to journey beyond self-pity
To a new awareness of You

To appreciate every experience
As Your gift of opportunity
To look at life anew
Teach me that I am not alone
For You are there as my faithful
companion
Always

'Do not be afraid . . .' I hear You say
Is it true You speak these words to me
This day?

Bless all who bring healing and wholeness
    into my life
May they know the strength and wealth of
    their presence

May I offer my pain
In union with all the suffering world
In some redemptive way
May I find purpose in pain

May all ills
Draw deep reserves of love and life
From all hearts who touch Your suffering
    face

May Your healing come
When I least expect
When my eyes can see
With deep respect
Your humble beauty
Manifest in the little ways
That touch my life with
Love.

PRAYER FOR THE LOSS
OF A LOVED ONE
THROUGH SUICIDE

Lord

I pray this night for all who grieve
Because their loved one has taken leave
Without warning
Without sign
Gone before their time

What sadness fills the heart
To cause a soul to thus depart
And leave so much behind?

Lord, there are so many questions
Unasked
Unanswered
Unknown
Why such loss
Should ever come
To many homes?

Lord
May Your Angel bring
Comfort in the endless night of sorrow
May a quiet peace settle
Within the hearts of those left behind
And in Your goodness
Can You stir a sign?
A treasured memory
A word of praise
A smiling photo
A friend's embrace
All reminding
We are not alone

May You call home
The one who has left us
To Your consoling arms
Where pain and sorrow
Are no longer known

May quiet understanding
Come to fill the vacant place
Where memory serves to ease the pain
And somewhere deep inside
Hope will bloom again
And when You look

Through Heaven's veil
On those now left behind
May soft tears fall
Like silver pearls
And ease the lonely mind

For in Your House
There is a room
Your promise to us all
A place of peace
A place of love
A healing place for all.

PRAYER FOR THE HEALING OF MEMORIES

L ord

I can not find the words
That I should say
Nor will I ever know the pain
Nor know the deep despair
Of souls who have been hurt
For lack of love and care

This is a prayer
A plea
That You would come
And gently heal
The souls of all
Whose hearts still bleed

Heal the silent scream
Of those who cry through nights and years
The child who forever weeps and wakes in
adult dreams

Heal the pain that never seems to fade
Replace with love the guilt of endless
shame

Hear the voice that longs to tell its tale
Hear the words where integrity prevails
Hear the truth where honesty has failed
Hear us now
We call upon Your name

Heal all hidden memories
In the deepest painful place
Suppressed through years of suffering
From memories erase
All thoughts of fear and failure
With tears that wash each face

You Lord
Were stripped
Bruised and beaten
Unprotected
So vulnerable
Derided
Mocked
Betrayed

And in the tomb
Where you were laid
We place
The hurt
The hate
The wounds of history

May we rise again
Through the power of your healing
      presence
To live
To laugh
To love once more

Send your Spirit
To move over all places of darkness
For our destiny is to be
People of the light
Waking from this night
To find you
In an early
Dawn.

PRAYER FOR REMEMBERING IN NOVEMBER

Lord

The harvest now is gathered
The meadows golden-brown
We rest before cold winter
The silent sheaves bow down

Barren trees cry leaves into the river
Yellow-red they fall
Floating on the water's edge
The lonely tree stands tall

An old raven perches
High above the church tower
And cries a lonesome sound
To the bells of Time

Now we remember
When life is gathered
And November winds blow

Memories to the fore
All the friends who sleep in death
I remember
More and more

How short is time
Lest we forget
Taking much for granted
For life is brief
From tree to leaf
A tiny seed once planted

Lord
May my memories
Always be happy ones
Of love
Of joy
That no time will destroy
For those who have died
Are gathered to You
Waking in light
In knowledge
In truth

May they tell stories
May they sing songs

In the Garden of Eden
All sadness gone

But they are as close now
A breath on the wind
May God show His mercy
To souls who have sinned

Where yew trees are planted
That catch autumn dew
Where heather is purple
And berries are few

So sleep dear souls in silence
Beneath the blue moon's gaze
Carved on weathered headstones
The years of waiting days

Waiting for You
O Lord.

PRAYER IN A TIME OF DECISION

L_{ord}

At various times in my life
I have known challenge
I have known change
Now is a time for decision
So I call upon Your name

I am weighed down with worry
My mind in constant flurry
What is right?
What is wrong?
The questions go on and on
I have gathered
I have sown
I have reaped
I have grown
I have wandered
Without certainty
Life shapes the edges and
Contours of the heart
There is much to discover

And much to impart
But I have heard a different song –
A different drum
Beating now
A different hum

Give me O Lord
The courage
To make this song my own
To nurture a seed now sown

How can I calm the fear
Whispering
Mumbling in my ear
Only fear breeds fear
It's hard to hear
Encouragement
When other sounds abound

May I make decisions
From a pure place in my heart
Knowing all goodness comes from You
Make doubt depart
Wisdom is not far
Beyond my reach
Lead me to that place

Where truth will speak
If I come to lose my way
And darkness still abounds
Will You call my name aloud
And search 'til I am found?

From all moments of anxiety
Set me free
From useless worry
Rescue me

For You are my courage
My wisdom
My guide
My life companion
In darkest night
May I entrust my decision
To You Lord
Knowing that what is good
Will not pass me
For all good things come from You

For restless is my heart
Until it rests in You.

PRAYER IN A TIME OF LONELINESS

Lord

I know that often You went
To a lonely place to pray
To find a way
Far from the madding crowd
Longing to be
Alone

On the other hand, Lord
I long to leave the wilderness
Of these vacant days
When silence is deafening
And hope goes astray
In the night of
A lonely heart

Am I the only one
Who feels this way?
Or are there others who
Pass the day

Dreaming they were
Someone else
Somewhere
Some day?

Behind the mask
I constantly wear
I cry inside
And hide in
Despair
Does Heaven really care?

Sometimes I hear
A voice within my soul
Reminding me – I am not alone
That You are on the road
Searching for me
Night and day
You will not stop
Until You have found the way
To my wounded heart

And when You do
Will I realise
That it was You
I have been missing

All this time?
Is it my heart that You search for
When You withdraw
To that quiet place?

You see and accept me
As I am
Though You are God
You are also truly
Man.

PRAYER OF A PRISONER

Lord

Beyond the window bars
There is a bird
Soaring
Diving
Swooping
Flying

A tiny bird
With a huge world at its wing

Here my world is tiny
And I cannot sing

Lord if You have really come
To set the prisoner free
Where are You now for me?

I have met myself so often
Within these walls
That enfold me
My heart can no longer hold me
I long to be free

Make my cell
A place where You would dwell
Despite my fall

Teach me Your compassion

You were once held in a prison
Before Your trial
And though innocent
You knew Your friend's denial
You walked the lonely mile
To a place on a hill
In the afternoon sun
You spread Your arms and died
And You brought a thief
To Paradise

Help me to forgive myself
Help others to forgive me
May I learn the journey
Far beyond this cell
To a green field in my heart
To a place of belonging
Where You are waiting
And trust will dwell

May I learn to contemplate
Your presence
My failures
Your blessings
My pain
Your promise of life and love

May I learn the gift
Of sacredness
In life
In others
In You

May I transcend
All weakness
All walls
All failures
All falls

Because You will never give up
On me, O Lord
Despite all
You remain
May tomorrow
Be a new day
Another day closer

Till I can take flight
A little bird
With tiny wings
Long before the
Night.

PRAYER OF A TEENAGER

Lord

It's difficult for me to pray
And I am not too sure how or where to
    begin
But I believe that I can be truly open and
    honest with You

My prayer is for a world
Where young people can live as equals
Without the concerns of
Image
Creed
Race
Beliefs

My prayer is for a world
Free from
Unemployment
Financial debt
Class segregation
Where every opinion matters
My prayer is for a world

Without
Loneliness
Addiction
Hatred
Violence
Torture
War

My prayer is for the courage
To change our world
To know that all of us
Make a difference

Help me in my times of confusion
When others reach out to me
And I reject them
Forgive my lack of tolerance
Especially when those older
Try to offer words of wisdom and
Encouragement
You Lord
Were once young and walked Your own
    way
But I am afraid to follow You
For fear of what You would ask of me
There are so many things

That place fear in my heart
I pray that I can bring them into the light
Out from the dark

I find comfort in saying these words to You
Knowing that You are there
And You do not judge me
Every effort I make
Is enough for You

I know that I will never
Be alone
When You are near
Encircle my fear

Bless my friends
With the same protection
Especially those who struggle with the pain
Of rejection
Of themselves
Of others

Encircle all of us
With Your light
Your love
Your presence

With Your eternal hope and promise
In us

May the world be a better place
Because we are born.

PRAYER OF THE ADDICT

Lord

I stand here on a distant shore
Alone
And hope has left her nest
And flown

Somehow
Sometime
Somewhere
I lost a sense of who I am

What was it that made me
Lose my reason
And drew me into these seasons
Of self-affliction
Habitual addiction?

In the beginning
I was drawn to the sweet perfume
Of distant desires
Now I know its fire
Burning deep inside

The unquenchable thirst
The brutal hurt

I know the lonely heart
Not my own
But of those who stand watching
From separate shores
Who wanted more
For me and now
I've gone too far

Is it too late
To believe that You are still there?
Despite my fall
Despite my all

I am the woman at the well
I am the man who once fell
At Your feet
And begged
If You want to, Lord You can heal me

Restore to me
All that time has lost
All that pain has cost

All moments past
All that I have wasted
Turn my loss to gain
That life might flower again

Untie the knots of my tangled life
All that is delusion
All the heart's confusion

May I find true courage
To rebuild the bridges
Once broken
Once destroyed

May I stand humbly
To seek forgiveness
From hurting hearts
That once held me
In loving care
Should I dare?

And in my ruptured life
May I see the light
Reaching through the chasms of despair
May love now settle there
Into that space

Once filled by painful pride
May You now hide
Restoring hope
Opening doors
To life anew

May I hear Your words
Once spoken with Your tears
To Lazarus Your friend of years

'Unbind him and let him go free' –
Would that You speak those words to me.

PRAYER OF THE REFUGEE

Lord

Your young flight into Egypt
Was captured on canvass
Written into Bible words
Told and retold
Through history
With angels
Dreams and mystery

My flight is unknown
But I too know fear
Voices at night
Scream in my head
Soldiers
Smoke
Silence

I look back
Running up a dirt road
My home in flames

My meagre belongings scattered to the
    four winds
The home of my children
Home of happy days
Home of God's ways
Destroyed

For days, for nights
I walk the miles
Hungry
Fearful and tired
Empty
Numb

I carry my child
Though heavy on my back
Not as heavy as the burden on my soul

My second boy has been taken
By rebels
What will he learn?
What will he see?
Shameful brutality

At twelve years
You were missing in the Temple

And Your mother searched for three days
Agony and ecstasy
He who was lost is found

My child too is missing
Will I find him in three days
Or spend the rest of my life
Looking around every street corner
For a boy-soldier?

With each day
Slowly the old begin to fall
Weak
Weary
Worn from war

Where are You, O God?
How can I dare to dream again?
I cannot cry
Like the parched earth
My heart is barren
Was Your mother weary
On her flight into Egypt?
Did she cry for nights over her baby?
Did the Bethlehem star continue to guide
them?

Tonight I sleep under the stars
Diamonds shining on sad eyes
Can You hear our pitiful cries

Lord
I have nothing
I am nothing
Only Your child

Lead me to fresh pastures
Like a true Shepherd
So that we will not want
Revive my broken spirit

Surround the heart of my son
And all children
With Your protection
Innocent minds
Smiling eyes
Not haunted lives
Tonight bless my sleep
I dream of a distant home
With a warm fire
A full plate
And peaceful heart
In the dark of night

I will light the lantern bright
And open wide the door
Should Your mother
Come once more
To seek her Son Divine
And bring me news of mine

So we can sleep in peace
With You
O God.

PRAYER ON THE DEATH
OF A CHILD

Lord

There is a garden where wildflowers grow
Where sometimes we would go
To pick bluebells in the spring

Wild lichens scent the air
And birdsong gifts the sky
Hiding in sun-kissed fields and hedgerows
Time would pass us by

Now I cannot hear the shrieks of pure
  delight
Nor the joyous sound of laughter
While blowing dandelions in the breeze
Now who will catch them after?

I am weary
Beyond the question
Weary from the bargaining

With life
With all
With You O God

Is Heaven such a place
That You need to fill it with beautiful
    children
While we are left behind
Searching for the sign
With hearts too numb to cry?

In my weeping comfort me O Lord
For You are tender
I am broken and need to know
That all is in Your care

Can I gather all the shattered pieces
Of tomorrow's hopes and dreams
Where love would grow
And we would hold
The treasure of our reaping?
Now all I see is an empty road
The skies are grey and weeping

Lord I am tired of asking why
Is there silence to my cry

Help me to know that You are there
To reach beyond despair
Give me the strength to rise again
When the stone is weighing heavy on my
    heart

Take the hand of my child
And go to the valley of the Angels
Where the wildflowers blow
And bluebells grow

Where
All is beauty
All is light
Would You wait for me there
In Paradise?

PRAYER TO THE ANGEL

Lord

I believe that You have given me an
invisible companion
To accompany me through life

Every breath, every secret thought, every
    action
Every word and every dream is laid bare
    before my Angel

May my Angel encircle me with light
May I hear his voice in the voice of
    conscience
May he illuminate my pathways
May he shelter me from the dark of danger
And reach me in the place of loneliness

May he shield my soul from all that would
    quench its light
Liberate me from limitations of fear
And open the doors of the hidden places of
    despair

May this holy companion fill my soul with
    Divine longing
Calling me into a new presence
Where You are forever new and beautiful,
    O God

May he stand with me at each threshold
Guarding my coming and going
Until that final moment
May he accompany me into Paradise
My eternal home and there
Place my hand in Yours Lord

O Angel of God
My guardian dear
Illumine my soul
That I might see
Your Heavenly presence
So close to me.

PRAYER FOR NEW LIFE

(in Celebration of Organ Donation)

Lord

You place in our hearts
The possibility of miracles
Allowing us the choice
To give the gift of life

Could my eyes become the windows of a
    new world
For one who has never seen the sun
To see in vibrant colour the beauty of each
    one
Who stands before them, radiant in their
    gaze?

Could my heart find a different rhythm
In life that knew despair?
For mine has loved and tasted
Would another ever dare
To take this heart and live again

Embrace a perfect day?
Give my limbs or muscle tissue
My kidneys or my lungs
To the child who longs for freedom
But cannot walk, or run

Let my blood run through the aging veins
Where life is ebbing slow
Bring hope where hope has faded
So dreams are dreamed once more

Take all that I can offer
So life may seize a chance
One soul to another
That You can watch them dance
For I have known Your blessings Lord
I've seen the sun arise
I've struggled climbing mountains
And yet through weary eyes
I have seen and tasted beauty
I have known its sacred kiss
Why should I then deny a soul
So much, that they might miss
The world You have created
The glory and the gift?

Lord
Give me the courage
To give and not to count the cost
For what is gained is all
But life and hope
What is lost is never lost.

This song is a song of remembrance for loved ones that are no longer with us in the earthly sense but will always live within our hearts. When we pray, they are especially close to us, as they are in Heaven where God dwells.

CHERE IS A PLACE

There is a time to remember, a time to
recall
The trials and the triumphs, the fears and
the falls
There is a time to be grateful for moments
so blessed
The jewels of our memory where love is our
guest

There is gold that is gleaming in a past we
once knew
In our tears and our laughter, 'twas love
brought us through
There's a road we have travelled where
sunlight has kissed
That carries us onwards when loved ones
are missed

There is treasure in our fields, there is
treasure in our skies
There is treasure in our dreaming from the
soul to the eye
For wherever we gather in the light of God's
grace

And for all whom we remember there will
  ever be a place

In the quiet of the evening, at the close of
  the day
We will rest from our journey, to the Lord
  we will pray
May we thank God for blessings for the
  moments we have shared
  As we look to tomorrow, close by us
  they'll stay

There is treasure in our fields, there is
  treasure in our skies
There is treasure in our dreaming from the
  soul to the eye
For wherever we gather in the light of God's
  grace
And for all whom we remember there will
  ever be a place.

This next song is based on the poetry of Thérèse of Lisieux. This French woman died at the young age of twenty-four and, though she lived a very simple and devout life, became a saint and a Doctor of the Church. She once wrote: 'I do not have the courage to look through books for beautiful prayers . . . I do as a child who has not yet learned to read, I just tell our Lord all that I want and He understands.'

JOURNEY OF THE SOUL

Journey of the soul where love will find a
  home
Journey of the soul to fill the heart with
  hope
And when the night seems far and when
  it's dark
Journey of the soul come and take me
  home

Forever and ever love will search my heart
Forever and ever lighting up the dark
Like a flame that's burning so my heart is
  yearning
To see the face of love

Refrain

Forever and ever in Your hiding place
Forever and ever love will be Your face
When I'm lost and all alone will You let
Your way be known
My Holy Destiny.

Refrain

This song is based on Michelangelo's beautiful Pieta where the Mother holds the Son in deep tenderness and love, and great sorrow. She reflects on the life of the child that she birthed and nurtured. Is there anyone who has held a child with more grief and love? How many other mothers will do likewise before the world learns to forgive and find true peace?

THE SILENCE AND
THE SORROW

Who'll come and share my sorrow
Hold my heart till I wake tomorrow
Is there a time that I could borrow
Oh, oh the silence and the sorrow

When I was young I dreamed of roads not
    taken
To walk the way so many had forsaken
And I would seek the heart of love's
    creation
It was found in You
When I was young I cried with tears of
    laughter
And deep inside I wondered what came
    after
How a heart could love without conditions
It was found in You

When love was young and living seemed
    forever

I knew somehow You never hid its
    pleasure
And all my tears uncovered hidden
    treasures
Love was found in You.

Angels in the Irish tradition have always been much revered. The word Angel in the Irish language is Aingil, which is derived from the words ain and geal meaning bright place – the place where these pure spirits come from. The song finds comfort in the closeness of our own personal angelic companion.

THE VOICE OF
AN ANGEL

When I'm lying in the darkness
And half-afraid to sleep
I keep thinking of tomorrow
And the thoughts that lie so deep
And I pray in talking whispers
'Cos I know that somewhere near
Is the presence of an angel
Come to hold me through my fear

And who are you who guides me
My messenger of light
Will you walk beside me now
Beyond the day and night
And who are you who guides me
With words I cannot write
It's the voice of an angel
The voice of an angel
The voice of an angel
Come to hold me close this night

When I close my eyes and open
The window of my heart
For I know that you will listen
Even though I kiss the dark
And as I'm slowly breathing
Oh the night just lingers on
I hear the voice of an angel
Come to calm me with a song.

Refrain

This song was written after one of the world's worst natural disasters – the great tsunami in South-East Asia, in my desire to comfort and console so many broken lives.

HOW CAN I HEAL YOUR BROKEN HEART?

See in disbelief, the face of untold grief
Crying eyes that seek the picture of a child
A life that seemed so long suddenly is gone
Lost by nature's crime and what is left to
  find

How can I heal your broken heart?
When all of the pieces are fractured apart
And though it may seem you're worlds
  afar
I pray you find someone, I pray you find
  someone
To hold you in the dark

And we wonder why and we wonder
  where
Oh where is Heaven now
In the midst of grief who will stand and
  weep
And share your tears somehow
Across horizons now

Refrain

And into the sky may your soul float on
   high
May the angels be your guide.

This song has inspired by the knowledge that in a world where injustice and brokenness abound, hope is found in the compassion of others and the belief that God hears all our cries.

ℎEAL US LORD

In our calling, stumbling and falling
Your truth dawning
Heal us Lord

In our yearning, searching, discerning
Wisdom, learning
Heal us Lord

Heal us Lord
Heal us Lord
Heal us Lord
May Your word renew us
May Your touch restore us
Heal us Lord

In division, hate and derision
Blinded vision
Heal us Lord

In hearts broken, harsh words are spoken
Empty tokens
Heal us Lord

Refrain

In our grieving, fragile believing
Hope receiving
Heal us Lord

In our rising, living and dying
Love abiding
Heal us Lord.

This next song is an invitation to the most wounded among us to find comfort, hope and belonging in the promise of Jesus.

COME TO ME

Come to me with all your burdens
Come and place your heart in mine
Come and tell me all your worries
My love for you will never die
For I am full of compassion
Do not be afraid
Come to me with all your burdens
I will never walk away

If you long for healing and your heart is
    full of fear
Listen to my promise in your searching I
    am near
If you are despairing and the darkness still
    abounds
I will give you comfort your heart I will
    surround

Refrain

If you are a stranger and you speak a
    different tongue
I will understand you, every voice I hear as
    one

Take my yoke upon you, come and rest in
   me once more
I will not desert you, my heart's an open
   door.

Refrain

THE LIGHT WITHIN

There is a secret hiding place within all of us. The Spanish mystic, Teresa of Avila, referred to this as 'the Castle of her Soul'. It is the place where no one can reach us, but it is also the place where God dwells. Many people do not know that such a place exists. Their lives can be very lonely and unfulfilled. Some try to quench this loneliness and longing in all kinds of ways that sometimes add more to their unhappiness.

One of the greatest illnesses of modern living is the pain of loneliness. We can be surrounded by great wealth, popularity and self-assurance, but deep inside we may be crying out in an isolating loneliness, cries that no one hears except ourselves. To sit with such aloneness can be a frightening experience. Many of us are afraid to be alone, so we fill our world with noise of all kinds to try and shut out the inner voice we hear. We cannot listen, because we find it very difficult to live with ourselves. Without our props, we feel exposed and vulnerable.

We think to ourselves that if we have to listen to God, our lives will have to change immeasurably, but that is because we do not know God, nor His love, nor His deep abiding concern for us. He wants nothing but good for us.

The voice that we hear within is the voice of our Creator. He made us out of love, and He comes to us in love. We were made for Him and, as St Augustine once reminded us, our hearts are restless until they rest in – and with – God. The loneliness we feel and so often try to fill comes about because we are without the presence of God in our lives.

God is the source of our longing, of our dreams and of our restlessness. Though we might believe otherwise, this longing will always remain with us until we can acknowledge God's calling deep within.

How does one recognise His voice? It is

born in the silence and will be heard in the silence. We may want to physically hear His words but we cannot, as God's voice is not a verbal communication. It is more profound, and will speak to us through actions, not in words. When we live shallow lives, our communication is superficial, but God's words to us are communicated on another level. They are rooted in silence and are a continuous invitation to experience His presence.

Once we come to know God and His ways, everything else becomes empty. His call will resonate forever. If we listen, we will hear Him when we least expect. It may be in the early morning, long before the dawn; in the midst of a hectic day; in the pleading of a poor soul; in the innocent eyes of our children; in the weary resting at day's end; in the quiet dreams that visit us in our sleep. We may hear His voice at any of these time and in any of these places.

And then He will call us to that secret place: the inner room and the light within.

PRAYER FOR CALM

Lord

In the midst of noise and hurry
Anxious days
Wearisome worry
Let me find Your peace

Let me journey
To a hiding place in my heart
My secret cavern
And find You waiting there

With every breath
May I know the serenity of silence
Where I am no longer
Dismayed by distraction

Take each care
Each worrisome thought
Each lonely road
Each battle fought
And place them in the sanctuary of Your
    care

May solitude befriend me
May I hear in the hidden depths
Your sweet voice echoing
And re-echoing a beautiful song of calm

May the invisible world
Become visible to my inner eye
And may Paradise open
A window to my soul

May I know that I am held
In safety
In love
In grace

May I be released from all that haunts me
May all that is lonesome in me find a
    tender home
May Your presence fall like gentle rain
On the hardened places of my heart

Lord
May every moment
Draw us closer

Until You and I become one
And only the breath of angels is heard
Come Lord let me know Your calm
You, my comfort and my balm.

PRAYER IN THE SILENCE

Lord

I want to go on a journey
To the hiding place of my heart
Prepare me to meet You
In the silence

Empty the chambers of all
Noise
Distraction
Negative attitudes

Gently take all anxiety
All useless worry
All free-falling thoughts
And replace them with Your calm

Take me into the stillness
With each breath
Draw me deeper into Your presence
Let me only know

Your peace
Your consolation
Your solace

For You know me
All my thoughts
All my words
All my dreams

You know the longings
Within the deep recesses
Of my heart

How poor I am
In Your presence
As I realise more and more
How little I know of You

I do not have adequate words
To honour You
Let my silence express
My love
My respect
My wonder

Let me offer to You
All I am
All I have
All I shall become

May I know that You
Are always there
Waiting
Quietly waiting
Any time
Always.

PRAYER OF FORGIVENESS

Lord

Help me to be humble
For I have wandered
Far from Your goodness and lived just for
    myself
Give me the courage to be self-effacing and
    honest

Forgive me for the times I have imprisoned
    myself
In selfishness
In greed
In envy
In arrogance
In anger
In despair
In mistrust

Forgive me for falling into
Self-pity
Self-doubt

Self-destruction
Self-containment

May these times of falling and failing
Lead me to a greater understanding of
    myself
And a new appreciation of Your infinite
    goodness and mercy

Unbind me
From the dark clouds that veil my life in
    fear
From the allurement of empty promises
From self-satisfaction
From the paralysis of self-loathing

To be humble
Is to come close to You
Who desires nothing more only
To love us as You do

Heal the deepest places of hurt
So that nothing is hidden from You
And the gaze of Your gentle eyes

In my sorrow
May I listen to the words of those

Who seek forgiveness from me
May I accept the sincerity of their hearts
So they too will know Your healing mercy
Through my pardon

Lord
Forgive my blindness
In failing to see Your abundant blessings
Given daily from Your kindness

Forgive me Lord
And let my shame now end

Forgive me Lord
That I would live again.

PRAYER TO JESUS

Lord

I come before You
In these sacred moments
Opening the shutters of my heart
That You would call the light into the dark
The secret cavern of my soul

If I tell You who I am
Will You shelter me
Beneath the firm arms of Your compassion
And gaze tenderly
Beyond the limits of my silence?

Who am I?

I am the son, the prodigal one
Returning from my journey
Of untold wrong
Where love was scarce
And temptation strong
Can You embrace me yet again?
I am the woman at the well

Tired and weary
Longing to quench my thirst
Drawing deep to find
Your truth as well

I am the blind one
By the Pool of Siloam
Can You stir the waters so I will see
Your gentle eyes
That find the light in me?

I am the weak one
Waiting for years
But I knew You would come
So I might touch the hem of Your garment
And live again

I am the curious one
Gathering to listen with the crowd
Bringing bread and fish
That You break and bless
And all become Your guests

I am the sinner
They all know my sins
I see the stones

My accusers bring
What words You write in sand
One by one I see them stand
And walk away
From what is written on each heart

I am Lazarus, friend
Wrapped in the cloths of death
When You saw me
You wept
You have called me from my tomb
And I will live again

I am Nicodemus of the night
Preferring dark to light
You have sought me out
I long for life

I am the little child
Who lies in fever's sleep
I hear You call beyond death's reach
'Talitha Koum'
Little one – come forth
Your voice is more beautiful than the
sweetest music
It resonates forever in my heart
I am all and I am more

I hear You knocking
On my door
Your lantern burning bright
Casting shadows where my life
Still seeks Your healing touch

Jesus
The beginning and the end
Jesus
I long to call You friend.

PRAYER TO MARY, MOTHER OF JESUS

Mary

I have always imagined you to be young
With serene beauty
Sun-kissed face that searched the heavens
With questions only answered deep
Within your heart
With great love you carried your child
Watching him grow 'neath the moon of
   Israel
And under Egypt's stars

You took the splinters from His dusty
   hands
Turning wood on Joseph's bench
And held Him close when He spoke of
   things
You could only carry in your heart

Did you know what lay ahead?
How He would heal the sick

Raise the dead
Find the lost and
See the hungry fed?
Little children would be well again
The blind would see
Lazarus would rise
And the lame run free

Did you know that your heart would
    break?
When He was bound and beaten
Hung upon a tree
For all the world to see
The sin of humanity

Did your heart almost burst
When you heard the tomb was empty?
Did you run to see
And cry again so many tears
Of joy?

In Heaven you do not age
And you are forever young
You are beautiful
Because you love

May we know that love
In protection

In affection
In direction
Just as you watched over your own Son
Watch over us

Help us to find
That pure place in our heart
Beyond cynicism
Beyond hate
Beyond fear

Turn your gentle face towards us
That we might listen to your Cana words
'Do as He tells you'

May we walk one day
When life is done
Through the fields of Paradise
Forever young
Enfolded in your mystery
O woman clothed in the sun.

In a world so often full of noise, it can be difficult to hear the voice of God but, in the silence, God reveals His beauty to those who seek it. This next song invites us to seek out the silence.

IN THE QUIET

When leaves are falling and the branches
    bare
Winter is calling and chills the silent air
When the moon is covered by shadows of
    the night
You will hear me calling if you come into
    the quiet

Be still oh be still for I am your God
Be still now and listen and you will hear
    my Word
Be still oh be still, deep within your life
For you will find me in the quiet

When souls are hurting and they don't
    know why
When hearts are broken and children have
    to cry
When prayers are spoken late into the
    night
You will find your answer if you come into
    the quiet.

Refrain

This song entreats us to live to be holy. For me, holiness is another name for humility. Only the humble heart can reveal the true face of God.

LIVE TO BE HOLY

Live to be holy
Live as if only
Someone is calling you
Deep in your heart
Live to be holy
Humble and lowly
And love will find you
And dwell in your heart

Where is the place that You go?
Where is there beauty to know?
When will the blossoms still send
Fragrance to the earth?
When will the stars start to shine?
When will the rain wash the vine?
Where will I hear Your sweet voice
Your beautiful voice?
When will the dove take to flight
And hide in the covert by night?
When will the winter be passed
So the scent of the flowers will last?
Set me like a seal on Your heart
Set me like a seal on Your arm
Where will I hear Your sweet voice
Your beautiful voice?

I have always been a great admirer of a ballad, a song that tells a story. In this ballad, various scenes in the life of the Virgin Mary are explored.

SING OF A LADY

Let us sing of a maiden, let us sing of a girl
Who spoke with an angel, sing yes to the
    Lord
Let us sing of a maiden, let us sing of a girl
Who bowed to the spirit and gave life to the
    word

So come and sing with me, we'll raise a
    joyful song
To lead the world from dark to light and
    turn to right from wrong
So come and sing with me a hymn of joyful
    praise
Ave Maria, Ave Maria, Ave Maria, the hope
    of all our days

Let us sing of a mother, let us sing of her life
Who searched for her boy child through the
    day and through night
Let us sing of a mother, let us sing of a sign
With Jesus at Cana to drink the new wine

Let us sing of a woman, let us sing of her
    tears
Who watched as they nailed Him, her love,
    to a tree
Let us sing of a woman, let us sing of her
    fears
Who held His face gently and washed Him
    with tears

Let us sing of a lady, let us sing of a crown
Who prayed in the silence as the Spirit
    poured down
Let us sing of a lady, let us sing of a crown
The hope of all people whose love here
    abounds.

THE LIGHT OF HOPE

In bygone days people often journeyed to holy places in search of a blessing for life, a connection with the Divine. They were drawn to these places by an awareness that was heightened by prayer, hoping that God would be revealed in some new way and that new insight would emerge. Such people were called pilgrims, and throughout the world they sought the holy ground of God's presence.

As we see with the pilgrims in Chaucer's *Canterbury Tales*, the lone pilgrim did not exist. Travelling on the medieval pathways and routes favoured by pilgrims, they depended on one another, engaging at different levels with their fellow travellers. Those in such groups would not normally have chosen each other as travelling companions, but people from all strata of society were found on the same road. To be a pilgrim was a call to be inclusive, accepting, forgiving and open. Very often, those travelling companions one pilgrim might have experienced as difficult merely reflected some facet of the same pilgrim's own personality.

As pilgrims, we go on a journey of discovery. Every step brings more opportunities to learn more about ourselves and about the revelation of God through life and through those who accompany us. It is also a journey to the heart, where one discovers the sacredness of one's own life and the meeting with God. When one discovers this relationship with God, healing and growth can take place. It is at this place of connection with God that change occurs. We hear the voice of God encouraging, advising and sometimes even warning us, when our lives have gone astray. Life experiences become more meaningful in the light of our encounter with God. But achieving this may necessitate going into the silence, in order to listen to our deepest feelings and needs.

The pilgrim sets out with an aspiration that he will never return to the same place or, even if he does, that he will never see it in the same light again. He opens his being to the grace of change and in doing so, leaves room for the possibility of God touching his life. This is the meaning of hope: reaching out into the future, not knowing what it will look like, but all the time believing in God's providence.

Today we too are pilgrims, in search of a deeper meaning to life. We are all searching for hope in a world that is constantly transforming, and not always for the good. Life has changed beyond recognition for so many in a relatively short time, as we begin to realise that houses built on sand may not always hold up. The old reliables of power and wealth are suddenly disappearing, leaving many broken lives in their wake.

We realise that we have choices to make. We can sit in despair or we can become people of hope. There is a Chinese proverb that says: 'Hope is like a road in the country: originally there is no road, but when many people walked a particular way, the road comes into existence.' This is where and how hope is born. Our belief in the God of mystery and miracles makes hope possible.

Today in life, there is little tolerance for mystery and miracle. The urban life, a life of mortgages, unemployment, poverty and racism, does not allow much room for belief in a supernatural God who cares for all. Yet when we stop believing, our capacity for hope diminishes, because then we limit the power of God to work in our lives. When we embrace humility, we allow room in our hearts for the miracle of God to happen.

We see the mystery of God revealed in so many beautiful ways. This is how hope is born. When we have hope in our lives, we can then offer the same to others who may live in the darkness of despair or the loneliness of loveless lives. God is beautiful and all that He offers is beautiful. When we allow ourselves the possibility of change, new beginnings are possible. Then one day, when we least expect it, the light of hope will appear in the early dawn, to forever light the way that lies before us.

PRAYER AT
CHRISTMAS

Lord

It's winter night
And the stars in diamond light
Shine into the dark
Seeking the place where You were born
One night long ago

On that night
I doubt that anyone sang
'Silent Night, Holy Night'
Nor was there a little drummer boy
To play till early morn
No coloured lights shone
On an evergreen tree
No baubles hung
For the world to see
Just some poor shepherd men
Fell on bended knee
Recognising the child
Born a refugee

There is Your mother
Wrapping You in swaddling clothes
Lulling You
Should the cold wind blow
To her breast she holds You tight

There is Joseph
His strong hands caressing You so warm
You would know no harm
Sleep in his gentle arms

But that was then and we are now
Still on the path to peace
Still praying for a night to sleep
Without war
Without pain
Without fear
Will You come again?

Lord
Come in the dead of night
When we least expect
Send a star so bright
To light
Your holy way
Come
Where You can find

A room
Within
Simple lives

In all we bring
To Your stable
In all we share
At Your table
Let us be humble
Or should we miss the innocent cry
Of a tiny child

May we learn the angels' song
May we climb the shepherds' hill
May we visit with the Magi
And on this night so still
May we welcome You Lord
So Your words can be fulfilled
'I will make my home in you'

As in Bethlehem
Just like the prophet said
Bethlehem*
The humble house of bread.

* *Bethlehem* – Beit Lehem *in Hebrew means 'house of bread'*

PRAYER FOR EASTER

Lord

The lilies are blooming in the fields
The hyacinths sway in the breeze
All of nature knows the greatness of this
    time

From the frozen winter
Life blossoms forth
Shedding the harsh cloth of snow
Paradise has kissed the earth
So all can know
The beauty of this time

The stone is rolled from the tomb
Death that we once knew
Is gone forever

We are not born to die
We are born for eternal life
With death comes not the dark
But the beauty of the Easter light

May I see in Easter time
The promise of eternal life
In every flowing stream
In every sunlight beam
In every field of green

In every evening sky
In every bird that flies
In every child that cries
In every living thing
Your Easter Presence

Lord
Roll away the stone
From broken empty lives
From greed
From hate
From lies
From hearts trapped within
The darkest night of nights
For all who live without a life

Let me run to the tomb
Before the sun's rise
Let my heart know surprise
To see before these eyes

The folded cloths
The shroud of suffering
Replaced by translucent beauty

Give me the joy of Magdalene
The first from history
To reveal the mystery
Of Your Resurrection

May her words re-echo
As once she said

That You are risen from the dead

Yes, Christ is truly risen
From the dead.

PRAYER FOR NIGHTFALL

Lord

The day is gathering to a close
And the night
Will soon be upon us

Let the layers of life
Blessed this day
By people, presence and place
Find rest 'neath the shadow of Your care

Renew, restore, repair
All promises broken or unfulfilled

Calm all angst and anger
So that we carry no hurt or hate
Into a restful sleeping

May each heart
Beat in rhythm
With every monastic prayer sung
Throughout this night
In chorus with the whole universe
In harmony with each star in each galaxy

In union with every voice of every angel
In all of Creation

May we dream dreams of
A healed world
Where no heart is gripped by
Fear or terror
Nor love destroyed
By human error

May the ease of sleep
Come to all who struggle
All who weep in lonely fields
All who toil with pitiful yield
All who yearn for hearts to heal

Surround us Lord
Surround us
So that we may surrender to sleep
Under Your watchful keep

May we wake to Your
Unfolding day
New moments of grace
Where we might glimpse
O Lord
Your face.

PRAYER FOR PEACE

Lord

This is a prayer for Peace
Not just empty words
But a real desire for healing of the heart

Grant us the ability to accept those
Who see the world
Through different eyes
Whose souls are dressed
In different guise

Give us the courage
To leave aside our arms
And see with honesty
What real destruction
Hatred, terror and fear
Achieves
And the legacy it leaves
Lord
It is difficult to turn the other cheek
When my future is consigned to the past
When restful sleep may never last

Who will heal the pain
Of mothers whose sons never come home
Of aged parents left alone
Of fearful children in bombed-out homes

Who hears the cry of the refugee
A tiny voice in the surging sea
Of humanity

Bless those who work for peace
Quietly humbly gently

Within and between nations
In communities
In families
In every heart
Lord may we know
Peace with justice
Peace with equality
Peace with forgiveness
Peace with compassion
Peace with humility
Help me not
To judge
To condemn

To seek revenge
To hate
Heal the hurts in broken lives and broken
　　hearts
Heal divisions that make us suspicious and
　　fearful
Heal bitterness that brings only pain

Help us to let go of the past
To find a peace that will last

May we see Your signs of hope
With Your eyes and Your heart
Let the rain wash the earth anew
So may we put our trust in You

Make me an instrument of Your peace
Until all is done
May we never cease.

PRAYER FOR PROVIDENCE

Lord

It is always so easy
To look for more
To search behind another door
The endless need to satisfy
As days and months and years pass by

But sometimes we need courage to stop
Count our blessings
Store life's lessons
In the sacred hold of our hearts

We have been given much
But we cannot see
For greed
For desire
For selfish vanity

Remove the scales from
Distant eyes

That we might see
And open wide
Our cluttered hearts
To offer praise

May we be always grateful
For life
Constant
Renewing
Each day with new surprise

For human goodness
In kind tender words
Hands
Hearts
Smiles

For colour
Not only in earth and skies
But in skin
And precious eyes

For love
The bridge from heart to heart
Lover
Child

Friend
Those near
And far apart

For choice
In many different ways
To feed
To clothe
To sing
To fill our nights and days

May we never take for granted
All that life affords
Poverty
Prosperity
A light or heavy load

May we remind ourselves each day
Of blessings we receive
The wonder of God's providence
Fulfilling all our needs

But somewhere there is hunger
And somewhere there is hurt
Would we hear the cries and turn away
Or try and quench the thirst

Perhaps Lord
You've given plenty
To few who have so much
That we might share from all we have
Become Your tender touch

In the places of the broken
In fields of shattered dreams
Where children go unwanted
Where life's not what it seems

But You are there, O Lord
In the midst of anxious fears
Queuing in the hunger lines
Crying tender tears

And we would hear Your voice
And the words remain unsaid
Who will turn and walk away
Or who will share their bread?

Help us to see Your face
In the face of all
So that their eyes
Can see into our hearts
And know we heed Your call

What You do for the least of these children
   of mine
You do for me

Lord, that we might see.

PRAYER FOR THE NEW YEAR

L ord

As I quench the lamp
And close the door on the past year
May I find the words of gratitude
To honour this passing time
The gift of Your design

For all that's come and gone
For decisions right and wrong
For unsung songs
I offer words of thanks

For days when life had plenty
For nights when hearts were empty
For undiscovered plains
When all was ventured but nothing gained
Through struggle and through pain
May we learn to rise again

Now at this threshold time
Make our hearts refined

To dreams new dreams
Beyond our own imagining

May we step into new places
Where courage will take us
Beyond our limited spaces

May we never lose the courage to seek
For a better world
Where no child will cry hungry
While another is bored with too much
Where war is remembered in hushed tones
A memory of forgotten days
Where colour and creed can celebrate
With pride, their different ways

And may Your gentleness, O Lord
Exude from every heart
May this New Year be a year
Of many blessings
Where new vision
Will transform the paralysed places
Of lonely hearts
Where we will discover
The hidden beauty of each soul
All who cross our pathways
And if we meet with sorrow

May we find an inner light
To guide us to the bright place
In the company of friends and family
In the company of love

May each moment of every month
Unveil Your abiding presence
In beautiful surprises
Re-awakening the child
Within each one of us

Lord bless us
And all we hold so dear
That You might guide the way
At the birthing of the year.

The Irish language includes many beautiful blessings for all facets of life. The following is a song of blessing on those whose company we have enjoyed and who take leave to journey home.

AS YOU GO

Can you see the lantern lighting in my
   heart
Lighting there for you to see though you
   journey far?
Can you see the shadow dancing on the
   moon
Bidding you to safely go so you'll be home
   soon?

As you go may your heart be strong
As you go may you know right from
   wrong
As you go and though you may grow tired
Know that I am with you, know that I am
   with you
Always by your side

Can you hear the children calling in the
   field
Rolling down the golden grass, night is
   drawing near?

Can you hear my promise, remember in
    your fear
As you go into the dark I am somewhere
    near?

Refrain

I have always loved the early Celtic writings. This next song is inspired by the 'Song of Amergin', in which the poet reflects on the Divine beauty of the wild Irish landscape.

if you Listen

When you're drifting like you're lost at
    sea
And you're helpless and your heart's not
    free
Just keep searching for your soul's desire
And you will find it if you reach inside
If you listen you will hear
If you listen I am near

For I am the wind that steers you when
    you sail
I am the breeze to warm the falling rain
I'll be your shelter when you reach the
    storm
I'll be your shelter, save you from all harm
When you're lonely and you feel alone
You need somewhere just to call your
    home
When you're weary and the mountain's
    high
And you struggle just to see the sky
If you listen you will hear
If you listen I am near.

In medieval times, it was customary to write Christmas carols using images and motifs from the natural world to depict the child Jesus. The image of a rose in December in this next song signifies vulnerability – beauty in the midst of the harshness of a cold winter.

ROSE IN DECEMBER

Sing me of a moon as it lingers to herald
    the new birth of the dawn
Sing of a bitter December when Heaven
    bids that love be born
So sacred the wind as it blows to places
    once barren and dry
Sing me of the stars in the heavens that
    gaze upon this humble child

Sing Gloria, sing Gloria, sing Gloria
So hear it well this tale to tell
Sing Gloria

Sing me of a rose in the winter still
    blooming though the night is so cold
Sing me of a sign in December as the
    mystery of love unfolds
How holy the words that we hear in
    history now hidden for years
Sing that we will always remember the
    wisdom of our God appears

Refrain

Sing me of a rose in December now
  blooming midst the winter snow
Sing me of a fragrance so perfect, the
  purest the world has known
And all who come to hear His name, will
  never know the world the same
Sing me of a rose in December, Emmanuel
  His holy name.

Refrain

ACKNOWLEDGEMENTS

*T*his book has come into existence because of the great desire of good souls to bring hope and healing into our world. I am indebted to the people who have made this possible.

My thanks, especially, to my editor Ciara Considine, who has been my constant guidance and inspiration for the past two years in writing this book. To all the people at Hachette Ireland who have been so kind and gracious in their support and belief in this project.

To Helen Whelan for her patience in helping with song manuscripts. To Bishop Jim Moriarty and all my colleagues in the

Diocese of Kildare and Leighlin for their affirmation and trust. To Mattie Fox for his guidance and advice. To Mark Cahill for his constant help and ear. To Leif, Cecelia, Kalle and all my friends in Sweden where this book began. To all my friends in the 'North' for their generous encouragement and support. To Fr John Dunphy and the people of Graiguecullen, Carlow, for their kindness and care. To the Poor Clare Community whose prayers and support are my constant strength.

To the many people who have inspired these pages and those who have journeyed with me through all the years, especially those who have used their own talents to enrich my life.

To my parents Tom and May, my family and friends, whose love keeps hope burning brightly in my heart.